World No. 1
My
Autobiography

BY
RIRISH PATEL

MAPLE
PUBLISHERS

World No. 1 - My Autobiography

Author: Rirish Patel

Copyright © 2025 Rirish Patel

The right of Rirish Patel to be identified as the author of this work has been asserted by the author in accordance with section 77 and 78 of the Copyright, Designs and Patents Act 1988.

ISBN 978-1-83538-518-0 (Paperback)
   978-1-83538-519-7 (Hardback)
   978-1-83538-520-3 (E-Book)

Book layout and cover design by:
   White Magic Studios
   www.whitemagicstudios.co.uk

Published by:
   Maple Publishers
   Fairbourne Drive, Atterbury,
   Milton Keynes,
   MK10 9RG, UK
   www.maplepublishers.com

A CIP catalogue record for this title is available from the British Library.

All rights reserved. No part of this book may be reproduced or translated by any form or by any means, electronic or mechanical, including photocopying, recording or by any information storage and retrieval system without written permission from the author.

The views expressed in this work are solely those of the author and do not necessarily reflect the views of the publisher, and the publisher hereby disclaims any responsibility for them.

World No. 1 - My Autobiography

My name is Rirish Patel and I am 47 years old, British citizen by birth and was born in London, UK. I am a Hindu, Indian. This is an autobiography of my extraordinary life which after reading you may well feel just like me, I am world no. 1 with all the amazing things I have done in my life.

I certainly was not rich ever but was a guy whose parents were ordinary working-class people (father supermarket cashier and mother factory worker).

Before I start writing my autobiography let me point out that I have done so many amazing things in my life that I may have forgotten some of the things I have done and hence not mentioned in this book but if you were to happen to meet me and ask if I had done something not mentioned in the book I will tell you. I have written everything I could remember at the time of writing this book.

I am not the richest man in the world but I am the world no. 1 because of all the amazing things I have done in my life.

Let's begin the journey of my life when I was at secondary school. I went on a skiing trip to Bologna, Italy but before I went on the school trip we went dry slope skiing in London to practise. At the dry slope centre in London we used the ski lift to go up the hill with our skis attached to our feet then once at the top of the hill we dismounted from the ski lift and took our positions at the top of the hill. We positioned our skis in a v shape pointing outwards to slow the speed down the hill, and then to go faster we changed the position of the skis from v shape to parallel skis and when near the bottom of the hill once again placed our skis in v shape to slow down. Now we knew how to ski. We didn't use hand ski poles. We were now ready for the Bologna ski trip.

In Bologna there was a lot of snow and we stayed in a ski resort there. The mountains were covered with snow, and again there were ski lifts to take us higher on the mountain because we were beginners. We didn't go too high up the mountain and ski in our 2-week trip.

There was also a gaming arcade machine centre in Bologna near the resort where I regularly played on the arcade machines.

In 1991, I went to South Africa to Johannesburg and Cape Town with a friend. We stayed in a 5-star hotel there. In Johannesburg I did a bit of shopping and bought a cricket bat. When we went to Cape Town it was a really sunny day and we realised that it was very close to the ocean. We stayed in a 5-star hotel called Cape Sun which had a swimming pool and Jacuzzi in the rooftop room which I used a lot during our stay. In Cape Town we also did a tour by vehicle on a table mountain which gave a spectacular view from high up of Cape Town and the ocean and shore beach.

Also in that year I went to Orlando, Florida and saw Walt Disney World which comprised Epcot Centre, Magic Kingdom and MGM studios. In Disney world they had monorail shuttles which I used a lot to go from one place to another in Disney world. Some of my favourite Disney world rides included Space mountain which was a capsule that goes round very fast like a rollercoaster ride, Star Tours which takes you on a star wars aircraft with motion movements as you look at the screen as you pass through the galaxy in Star Wars adventure, The Twilight Zone Tower of Terror which takes you up a lift at great height and drops you as if the lift is broken, Pirates of the Caribbean, Splash mountain which is a ride on a log in water surroundings and where you drop from height from a waterfall. It's a small world which is a musical water ride which goes through all the continents and their cultures, etc.

I also went to Universal studios which is so awesome and some of my favourite rides include E.T. Adventure in which you sit on a bike with E.T. towelled in basket in front of you as you pass through in the world, Earthquake which is for that movie in which you are in a train and suddenly come to stop at the start of an earthquake and everything falls apart in front of you, Jaws from the movie in which you are in boat and confronted by jaws throughout, Back to the Future: The Ride in which we travel back in time and then in the future in Marty McFly's time machine car with a lot of motion in this ride, etc. I also went to Sea world and really enjoyed the Shamu show. Shamu is a large killer whale who does all kinds of tricks in which Shamu is in an enormous enclosed water cylinder and you get wet if you are at the front row seats. There are sea lion, walrus, dolphin, penguin shows there too and many other sea animals performing. One of my favourites at sea world was where there is a water show in a make-believe hotel and the sea lions do all kinds of funny things with the host and other animals. I also went to Wet n Wild water park in Orlando which was an amazing water park. I also visited Busch gardens in Tampa bay which had many rides I went on.

Then I went to New Jersey.

I also went to New York and rode in a limousine for the very first time and I sat in the back seat behind the chauffeur. The limo had a fridge, tv, etc which was amazing and I went up on the twin towers before it was destroyed on 9/11. One of the towers of the twin towers was a business centre and not open to the public and the other tower, visitors could go up on. It was amazing to have ever gone up the twin towers as subsequently it was destroyed by terrorists. I also went to Washington DC and saw everything there including US mint money making manufacture and Lincoln memorial and Washington monument and the White House. I also went to Tijuana, Mexico. I crossed the border then came back to the USA.

I went to Orlando 3 times, once in 1991, then 1994 and again in 2002.

In 1994 I went to Orlando and New York and again went up the twin tours in New York.

In 1997, I went to the USA, Los Angeles and Disneyland, and some of my favourite rides there included Big Thunder Mountain ride where you are in a wagon and zooming in a rollercoaster ride around desert and mountainous surroundings. Space mountain as already discussed is similar to Orlando. It's a small world, Splash mountain, Star tours, Pirates of the Caribbean, Disneyland railroad, etc. and Universal studios in which my most favourite ride was Jurassic Park: The Ride. Other rides there included 'Back to the future: The ride', etc. I also saw the Hollywood walk of fame with famous people's names on the star studded walk and I saw Hollywood Boulevard with many shops and the Hollywood sign there.

In October 2002 my best friend and I flew on a Concorde return from Heathrow to New York in 3 and a half hours' flight time. This was the fastest supersonic plane ever built. At Heathrow airport we went into the Concorde room to wait for our flight to depart. It was an exclusive room only for

Concorde passengers. We took a chartered plane to Orlando and spent 2 weeks in Orlando and then flew by chartered plane from Orlando to New York and flew back home on Concorde from New York. Concorde retired soon after in the following year and I was fortunate to have been one of those people to have ever flown on it.

In 2005, I went to USA and Canada with my parents to San Francisco and saw Golden Gate bridge and Alcatraz prison on the island, and Seattle in which I went up Space needle tower, and Chicago and Las Vegas where I entered one way into a casino strip and saw game machines, people playing roulette and playing card games, etc and when I came out of the casino strip in Las Vegas my helicopter was waiting for me to start my Grand Canyon by helicopter tour in USA. I sat at the front in the helicopter and we started our Grand Canyon tour. We passed through the Grand Canyon with the tour guide explaining and then landed on a helicopter pad at the end of the Grand Canyon journey and made our way on horseback to the hut for food and drink. Afterwards we headed back by helicopter through the Grand Canyon to Las Vegas. In Canada I went on a helicopter ride to see Niagara Falls and the view was spectacular and on the Maid of the Mist boat ride for a close up of Niagara Falls and went up CN Tower in Toronto. In both the helicopter rides I sat at the front next to the pilot.

I have been to see Taj Mahal, with my parents, which is considered one of the wonders of the world. It was commissioned by the Mughal emperor, Shah Jahan to house the tomb of his favourite wife, Mumtaz Mahal. The building was so big and beautiful, and the surroundings were well maintained. I have also been to Bombay in India.

In 2006 I went on the Queen Mary II cruise ship from Southampton to New York, it was the first time I had travelled in a cruise ship. It was an enormous and spectacular cruise ship. When it set sail the Atlantic Ocean was calm but a couple of days later the ocean became rough and the cruise ship was rocking back and forth. I had my own room onboard and there on the ship I would regularly sit on the side of the ship, indoors and watch the ocean. There were tables set for our breakfast, lunch and dinner. I also went on the deck of the ship when the ocean was calm to view the ocean surroundings. I also did some shopping on the cruise ship. When I got off at New York I went by limousine to my hotel and the next day I went up to the Empire State building and also saw the Statue of Liberty. Unfortunately, the Statue of Liberty was closed for viewing that day so I could not go up it. I flew back from New York in a British Airways first class seat.

In 2008, I went on a 5-day Europe tour to Belgium, Luxembourg, Germany, Switzerland and France by ferry and then a coach tour. There I went to Brussels and did a city tour and went to "Atomium" and then got onboard our coach to Luxembourg and did sightseeing there. The next day we drove to Black Forest in Germany to see where the cuckoo clocks are made here and I also purchased a small cuckoo clock as sovereign and relaxed by the lake, then went by coach to Switzerland to the majestic Rhine falls. I re-joined our coach to go towards central Switzerland to Lucerne. In Lucerne I spent time admiring Lake Lucerne and took a wonderful walk around the Old Town in the pretty cobbled streets and saw the Chapel Bridge and the Lion monument. I ascended 10,000 ft to the summit of Mt Titlis and took a small cable car before I boarded the world's first revolving cable car, the Titlis Rotair. At the summit I enjoyed the panoramic views of the Swiss landscapes and I walked the highest cliff walk, a suspended pedestrian bridge along the cliff of Mount Titlis. Then we got on board the coach to drive to Interlaken where I spent time shopping and on to Geneva, did sightseeing there. The next day we headed out to Paris and embarked on the famous "Bateaux" cruises of Paris for one-hour cruise along the River Seine and then we did a city tour of Paris and also went up the Eiffel tower.

In 2009 I went to Dubai and saw Burj Khalifa but it was still being constructed and wasn't ready for visitors. I went on Dhow cruise where in the evening I cruised along the banks of the historic Dubai Creek where the Dhow Cruise combines the best of culinary delights and stunning views of old and new Dubai. I also went on a desert safari. The safari takes you to a thrilling fun-filled evening you will never forget. Leaving the hustle and bustle of Dubai, the desert safari guide took me in a 4x4 vehicle for an exciting and thrilling journey rolling over the dunes. The experience of going up and down the desert pumped my adrenaline with excitement which was amazing and I also enjoyed a scintillating belly dance performance. We also went to a water park near the 7-star hotel, Burj Al Arab.

In 2010, I went on holiday with my parents to Kenya and saw Maasai Mara game park where we saw prides of lions eating their kill - elephants, giraffes, hyenas, cheetah, leopard, wildebeest, buffalos, impala, etc and Lake Nakuru where the flamingos are. In Lake Nakuru we had an incident. Our Safari van driver parked up a bit of a distance away from the lake and we got off and headed towards the lake to see the flamingos. After about 10 minutes my mum said, "I see a rhino coming," and so I quickly shouted "Run," and me and my parents ran to our van with me shouting, "Run quickly, rhino," all the way. We just got in the van and closed the door; the rhino was right next to our van! It was a close call, we could have got killed that day by a rhinoceros. We stayed in a tent overnight with electric fencing around the perimeter to deter wildlife coming into the perimeter. In Kenya we did golfing in the resort and swimming in the hotel's pool and I also rode a horse in Kenya.

In 2011, my parents and I went on holiday to Australia where the tour included Perth, Ayers Rock, Alice Springs, Cairns, Sydney and Melbourne. There was a lot of trekking in Australia and it was amazing to see the beautiful Australian surroundings on foot. I saw the Australian native kangaroos there and a koala. I went on a seaplane in Sydney where I saw the Blue mountains, past the Three Sisters rock formation. We also went to Bondi Beach and I did the walk on Sydney harbour bridge. I went inside the Sydney Opera house, and hot air ballooned across the outback. I threw a boomerang correctly and it came back to me. I saw the major cricket grounds and Tennis arenas in Sydney and Melbourne and saw Uluru in Ayers rock.

In Alice Springs I saw the flying doctor base and the famous school of the air sightseeing. I snorkelled in the Great Barrier Reef and saw among others, a puffer fish. A cable car ride to Kuranda rainforest in Cairns, Skyrail, and railway train. Kuranda rainforest is famous for the Cassowary bird, although we didn't spot one. They can be dangerous and are known to have killed human beings. When in Melbourne we went to Philip Island to see the penguins come onto the shore from the ocean at night. It was an amazing experience and when we were going back from our seats to the coach the penguins were on the stairs and across the land.

In 2012, my then 4-year old son, Yash, and I went to Egypt on holiday. It was the first time Yash had gone abroad. I went to Cairo and saw the Great Pyramids of Giza and also went inside a pyramid and saw the Sphynx (a mythical creature with the head of a human, a falcon, a cat or a sheep and the body of a lion with the wings of a falcon). We went on an overnight sleeper train from Cairo to Luxor and visited the Valley of the Kings in Luxor including Tutankhamen's and Ramesses' tombs. We then took a flight to Aswan and did a boat cruise across the longest river in the world, river Nile. We visited many Egyptian temples there. In Egypt, we also went on a camel ride.

I have been on the Eurostar train about 3 times - once to Disneyland (Marne-la-Vallee), another time to Paris and on a return to Brussels.

After coming back from Egypt, I went to Italy by myself on a tour package. I visited the Vatican City, home to the Pope and the Roman Catholic Church, and then I proceeded to view Trevi Fountains, arguably the most beautiful fountains in all of Rome. The next day I went to see the Colosseum, once home to the gladiators. I saw the Leaning tower of Pisa and went on a Gondola in Venice and visited Milan too, which is renowned as one of the design and fashion capitals of the world.

In 2013, my parents, my son and I went to Spain on holiday. I went inside Barcelona stadium and Real Madrid stadium on a stadium tour. I went to the largest aquarium in Europe in Valencia. I visited Barcelona, Madrid and Valencia cities, and also a couple of beaches in Spain. I saw a live bull fight in the ring in Spain and I went on a speed boat ride in Spain.

In 2014, I went to Disneyland Paris by ferry with my parents and son and saw the Eiffel tower. Some of my favourite rides included Ratatouille in which you are made to believe you have been shrunk to the size of a rat, also Big Thunder Mountain Railroad, Crush's coaster which was a very fast frightening ride, Pirates of the Caribbean, Star Tours. It's a small world, Space mountain and Disneyland railroad.

In the same year I saw the northern lights in Scandinavia. There I rode a sleigh attached to Huskies dogs, a reindeer sleigh ride, and drove a snow mobile bike. I realised when in Scandinavia that you cannot see aurora borealis with the naked eye but only via camera and saw the northern lights there whilst on a northern lights forest trek. We wore snowshoes on our trek. I stayed overnight in an igloo. I also went to the Isle of Wight for one day.

In 2018, I went to Scotland on a tour package. We departed by coach from London to Glasgow. The city sightseeing included Glasgow Cathedral, Georges Square, the university and the city chambers. The next day we visited Loch Lomond and later drove to Fort William to visit the Nevis Range and I went to the very top of Nevis mountain by cable car. We also had a photo stop at Commando Memorial & Neptune's Staircase. The next day we drove to Edinburgh, en route, to a photo stop at Falkirk Wheel. Then we visited The Kelpies, 30-meter-high horse-head sculptures depicting Kelpies and finally we arrived at Edinburgh and visited the famous Edinburgh Castle and later drove the Royal Mile to see St Giles' Cathedral. On the last day we departed for Lake District and enjoyed a scenic cruise on Lake Windermere and then made our way back to London.

In 2019, I went to Dubai to see Burj Khalifa, the tallest building in the world. I went up Burj Khalifa each day on the 4-day tour. I also did tea in the clouds on the top floor of Burj Khalifa and enjoyed eating cakes and having tea and coffee in the afternoon. I had a really good experience of Burj Khalifa, visiting it in the morning, afternoon and evening at sunset on separate days. I also went to Dubai mall and visited the Dubai Aquarium and underwater zoo, which includes the world's most extensive collection of sand sharks and one of the world's largest acrylic panel viewing platforms. I viewed numerous marine habitats here, including an underwater tunnel house of 33,000 aquatic animals, from crocodiles to tropic fish. At night, I enjoyed the musical fountains.

Also in 2019, I went to Goa in India. I got off at Dabolim airport and took a prebooked minicab to my hotel. The driver said they also offered sightseeing tours of Goa. So I took the offer and booked a Goa tour with them.

I flew to Gujarat from Goa, and one day I went to Kevadia to go up the Statue of Unity, the tallest statue in the world. The Statue of Unity is next to the Sardar Sarovar Dam which I also saw close up. I went up the Statue of Unity in a lift and saw the spectacular view of Kevadia from high up.

In January 2022, I went to the exotic Maldives with my wife on our honeymoon. We took a speed boat from Maldives airport to our island resort. On a dolphin tour, we saw dolphins in the water from the boat up close. I paid for an all-inclusive package for our trip and drank lots of mocktails there. As we told the resort that we are on honeymoon whilst we were on the dolphin tour they decorated our room and put a non-alcoholic corked bottle drink in an ice bucket in our room and our bed was decorated with flowers in a heart shape. We had a Jacuzzi outside the ocean front too and a wooden sunbed to relax and enjoy the ocean. There was a staircase outside to walk down to swim in the beautiful ocean. The resort had white sandy beach and crystal-clear waters, rich in dissolved minerals which act as a mirror reflecting the sky's azure tones. We stayed 4 days in Maldives and thoroughly enjoyed our honeymoon in the resort. It was the best resort I could possibly have chosen for our honeymoon.

In September 2022, my wife and I went to Snowdonia, which is the tallest mountain in Wales, and were amazed by the beautiful surroundings and greenery. We went on Snowdon railway to go up Snowdonia mountain and once at the top of the mountain got off to admire the surroundings on this amazing mountain.

In November 2022 my wife and I went to India for about 3 months. We attended Arijit Singh's concert in Ahmedabad. He is one of my favourite Indian singers and sang many songs in the concert including "Deva Deva" and "Kesariya" to name two which were from the Bollywood film "Brahmastra". I also went to the largest cricket ground in the world, Narendra Modi stadium, to see the India vs New Zealand T20 match in which Gil hit a century for India, taking India to victory. It was amazing in the stadium with India supporters singing "Jite ga toh jite ga, India jite ga" and some supporters coming on to the ground playing dhol (drum).

When my wife and I went to India again in October 2024, for a month, we attended a Falguni Pathak garba, a singer, named as the "Garba Queen". We also went to a Kairavi Buch garba during Navratri and spent Diwali and Indian new year there, and enjoyed fireworks including the UK banned 5000 firecrackers and "sutli" bombs. I also saw "Bhool Bhulaiya 3" a Bollywood film in the cinema on opening day, 1 November 2024.

Academically, I had 5 GCSEs grades A-C, 2 A levels grade C and D in 2 subjects.

I went to Kingston University in 1996 to do 3 years' BSc in Joint Mathematics and Statistics and got a 1st Class degree. I studied ACCA and passed 6 papers out of 14 to qualify but gave up as accountancy wasn't for me. I did an IT course with a skills training home study provider in August 2007 and attained A+, Network+ and Cisco CCNA and Cisco CCNP in 18 months. I was now a Cisco Network Engineer ready to work in the industry as one. I did various IT contracts with IT companies from 2014 to 2018. When I was not in IT I was working in retail, hospitality, etc with agencies.

I passed my driving test for the first time in 1996. At that time there was no theory test and only a driving test was required to get a driving licence.

I want to talk a little about my married life too. I married my first wife in November 2006 and had a son, Yash, with her but since this marriage did not work I separated from her in January 2010 and got a divorce in December 2010. When she separated from me she left with my son but was incapable of caring for my son and so the social worker gave my son to me in April 2011 and then my parents and I took care of my son. There were court cases for custody and contact but my son remained with me and he also did not like his mother and her family. My ex-wife was stalking me on Indian marriage websites and trying to remarry me which was never going to happen. In May 2016, she turned up outside my house knocking on my door to see our son as contact was stopped because of my son's unwillingness to see his mother. I got provoked by her as I was at home at that time and I attacked her in annoyance. I was taken into police custody and imprisoned for 3 years on charges of grievous bodily harm (GBH).

Although this was never planned for in my entire life, I have been in prison too. I was initially taken to Category B prison, Wormwood Scrubs. Considering my good behaviour in prison I was taken to Category C prison, Brixton prison, and after another 6 months of good behaviour, transferred to open prison, Ford, which is also known as Category D prison, where I spent my remaining time in prison before being released on licence at half way stage (18 months). On release from prison I was put in a probation hostel with curfews which I abided by. I had to see a probation officer every week.

I remarried a wonderful woman, Drashti, in August 2020 who had a child from her previous marriage. My step daughter's name is Prisha.

Now let's talk about the events and things I have done in the UK.

I went to see all the Wembley stadium matches in the Euro 96 championships. I used to regularly go to England friendly football games at the old Wembley stadium and remember one extraordinary game when England played Colombia in 1995 where the Colombian goalie, René Higuita, did a scorpion kick to clear the chance off the line. I have even seen Tendulkar bat when I went to see the England vs India test match at Lord's cricket ground in 1996.

Lord's, Oval, Old Trafford and Edgbaston cricket grounds in the UK were my regular haunts.

In 2005, I went to Old Trafford for the very first time to see my team, Man Utd, play AC Milan. Man Utd lost the first leg at Old Trafford 1-0 and ended up getting knocked out.

In 2011, I also did a tandem skydive in the UK and when we were about to hit the ground we had to push our legs forward and land on our bum. It was an amazing experience to see the UK from the sky but at times I closed my eyes as I was a bit scared.

In 2006, I went to see the Masters snooker final between Ronnie O'Sullivan and John Higgins at Wembley Conference Centre which John Higgins won. I also went to see the London 2012 Olympics and Paralympic games. My son and father also came to some of the games. I went up the Orbit tower which was in the Olympic Park in Stratford. In the Olympic games I saw 100m round 1 races where I saw Usain Bolt race for the very first time. My seat was excellent, right next to the track and I saw Usain Bolt race close by.

I also saw Anthony Joshua win gold in the final of Super heavyweight boxing and my seat was very close to the ring. I saw team GB beat UAE 3-1 in the football group stage at Wembley stadium and the London 2012 Football Olympics Final between Brazil vs Mexico at Wembley stadium in which Mexico won the gold medal. I went to Wimbledon and among others saw Roger Federer and Andy Murray play in the first round, and Djokovic was beaten in the bronze medal match by Del Potro.

I went to the opening ceremony of the London Paralympics, 2012 at Olympic stadium in which Stephen Hawkins came on and talked, and Rihanna performed her song Umbrella in spectacular style. I also went to the closing ceremony in which Coldplay played in spectacular surroundings with panels in front of the seats for an image show throughout and I loved Coldplay's performance "Viva La Vida". Jay-z and Rihanna also came on. I saw swimming in the aquatics centre and cycling in the Velodrome, various events in Excel including weight lifting. My son and I went to the Royal Artillery Barracks to see the archery and air rifle events. We did some archery on the target there and I tried my hand in the air rifle at the range. I went to the Olympic stadium to see various races at the stadium.

I also did Bungee jumping in London near the O2 arena in North Greenwich.

In 2013, I heard a famous Indian singer, Shreya Ghoshal, sing at Royal Albert Hall, with my mum. She sang many hit songs including "Teri Ore".

November 2014, I went to see Argentina vs Portugal at Old Trafford, Manchester to especially see Messi play live for the first time and also Cristiano Ronaldo play. Portugal won the match 1-0. I drove to Manchester and back in my Honda Accord iVTEC car to see the match. I went to the London Eye on 31 December 2014, for the New Year's Eve fireworks display.

In 2015, I went to see the Rugby World Cup in London. I went to see New Zealand vs Argentina at Wembley stadium, England vs Australia at Twickenham, Rugby World Cup semi-final between New Zealand vs South Africa at Twickenham and the Rugby World Cup final, New Zealand vs Australia, at Twickenham stadium. In the final New Zealand won an epic match by 34-17 against Australia. Jonah Lomu watched his beloved New Zealand win the World Cup at Twickenham but died a few days after. In the same year I saw Usain Bolt win 100m at London stadium in the anniversary games in 9.87 seconds and my seat was next to the track, affording me an excellent view.

In 2016, I went to see a UFC fight in O2 Arena between Michael Bisping and the legendary Anderson Silva, which Bisping won. Also that year I went to Shakespeare theatre in

London for the very first time and saw the play "Macbeth" and "Imogen" and also, "The Winter's Tale" at Sam Wanamaker Playhouse inside Shakespeare Globe theatre.

I went to see two matches in the 2016 PDC World Darts Championships at Alexandra Palace and saw the legendary Phil Taylor play in his opening match and win and also saw defending champion Gary Anderson win his semifinals match. I also saw him throw a nine-dart finish in his semifinal against Jelle Klaasen

In 2018, I went to Tottenham Hotspurs vs Barcelona group stage game at Wembley stadium to see Lionel Messi play. Messi played unbelievably well and scored 2 goals and Barcelona won 4-2. Also, that year I went to see the Women's Hockey World Cup at Lee Valley Centre in Stratford and bought tickets to see every competing team once in the group stages including brilliant and eventual winners Holland, also India, England, Australia, New Zealand, etc with excellent seats to see the matches. I also went to see a track cycling event in the Velodrome. I heard Ann-Marie at Roundhouse, she performed her hit single "Rockabye" which I love and "Ciao Adios" which is another favourite of mine and "Perfect to Me"; Ed Sheeran at Wembley stadium and he performed his hits like "Castle on the Hill", "Perfect", and "Galway Girl"; Bruno Mars at Hyde Park where he performed classics such as "Just the Way You Are", "24K Magic" and "Marry You";

Mariah Carey at O2 arena where she performed her songs such as "Always be my Baby", "When you Believe", "Honey" and "The Star"; Rita Ora where she performed on stage one of my favourite songs "I Will Never Let You Down" and others at Ascot Racecourse and Disney on Ice at O2 arena and "Harry Potter and the cursed child" in the theatre. I also saw the Challenge cup final rugby match and charity shield 2018 at Wembley stadium.

That year my parents and I went to Shakespeare theatre to see the play "Hamlet". About 3 weeks later I went by myself to see the play "Othello" and later that year I went to Sam Wanamaker playhouse to see the play "Macbeth".

On 30 June 2019, I went to see the first ever MLB game to be staged in the UK at London Stadium, New York Yankees vs Boston Red Sox. My seats were excellent and I wanted the Yankees to win which they did, wrapping up the series 2-0. Craig David sang for pre-match entertainment.

In 2019, I went to see the cricket World Cup which was held in the UK. I went to see England vs South Africa, India vs Australia, England vs Australia and India vs Pakistan in the group stages and England vs New Zealand in the Cricket World Cup Final 2019. The tournament began on 30 May between England vs South Africa which England won with that amazing catch by Ben Stokes at the Oval cricket ground. I also went to see India vs Australia at the Oval and being an

Indian I was obviously looking forward to seeing India play and win, which they did as Shikhar Dhawan hit a century.

The match I was really looking forward to seeing in the group stages was India vs Pakistan at Old Trafford in Manchester in which Rohit Sharma hit a century for India. I was shouting and cheering for India to beat our bitter rivals Pakistan, which they did with rain on Duckworth-Lewis-Stern method. To see this match, I took Virgin trains from London to Manchester on the day before the match, stayed in a hotel and went the next day by Uber to the ground. It was amazing to see the excitement of the supporters outside the ground. India has so far never lost a World Cup 50 overs game to Pakistan.

I also went to see England vs Australia in the group stage at Lord's cricket ground. England lost the game making them nervous about remaining games to qualify for knock out stages.

If someone would ask me, 'who do you want to win the World Cup - India or England', I would say to them I love India as I am Indian, but I want England to win the World Cup because they are hosts and have never won the World Cup before and I was born in the UK.

Then came that super over World Cup Final at Lord's which I was thrilled to see. During the World Cup all my seats were excellent viewing seats.

I sat in my seat to watch England vs New Zealand in the World Cup final. New Zealand batted first and I stayed until 45 overs and then went for food and drink. I returned to my seat before England started batting and watched everything unravel from there onwards. It ended up 241 apiece and went on to a super over. No-one had heard of anything like it in a World Cup final, it was a unique first time ever and even the super over was level and England won on boundary count. I cried when Jos Buttler knocked off the stumps to run out. Knowing England had won their first World Cup ever and being born in the UK meant so much to me. I had bought so many Cricket World Cup 2019 sovereigns including cups and caps.

In 2019, I went to British Summer Time at Hyde Park to see Celine Dion live in concert. I loved her songs "I'm Alive" and "My Heart Will Go On".

I went to Spice Girls concert in the same year at Wembley stadium in their reunion concert in which they performed the hits "Mama", "Spice up Your Life", "Wannabe", "Viva Forever", "2 Become 1" "Too Much" and "Who Do You Think You Are". I was singing and dancing along to their classics and Ariana Grande at O2 arena. I like her song "One Last Time" and James Arthur concert at Eventim Apollo, London. I like many of James Arthur's songs including "Rewrite the Stars" and "Say You Won't Let Go" and I saw Little Mix concert at O2 arena where they performed their songs including "Black Magic" which is one of my favourites and "No More Sad Songs" too and many other classics.

I went to see the Women's FA Cup Final in 2019 at Wembley stadium too.

I went to see the charity shield football match in 2019 between Man City vs Liverpool,

my first ever American football, NFL, match at Wembley stadium between Jacksonville Jaguars vs Philadelphia Eagles which the Philadelphia Eagles won. My seats were right at the front on level 2, excellent view. I went to Giants Live at Wembley arena in 2019 to see the strongest man competition.

In 2021, I went to see the Euro 2020 Final at Wembley stadium in which Italy won on penalties against host England after finishing 1-1 AET. The same year my wife, Drashti, and I saw the play "Romeo & Juliet" at Shakespeare theatre.

In 2022, I went to see the Women's European Championships in London. I saw Germany vs Denmark at Brentford stadium with my wife and Spain vs Denmark at Brentford stadium with my son. Me and my son and I saw the Women's Euro 2022 Final at Wembley Stadium which England won against Germany, England 2-1 Germany AET, and it was the first major trophy the Women's team have ever won in their history.

In 2022, I went to Birmingham 2022 Commonwealth Games with my wife, Drashti and by myself to see mixed doubles badminton in which Malaysia beat India. Another day I went with my wife to Birmingham 2022 to see squash being played.

We only saw 3 Commonwealth games and the last one my wife and I went to in Birmingham in 2022 was the best - Women's India vs Australia in the Birmingham 2022 commonwealth games cricket final at Edgbaston cricket ground in which Australia batted first and made a huge score and India fought well to go close to winning but fell short.

In October 2022 my wife and I went to see England vs Uganda playing netball at Copper box in London in a friendly which England won. I did a face paint with England's flag on both cheeks at the stadium.

I saw Tyson Fury knock out Wilder in their Wembley stadium match in 2022.

In 2022 my wife and I went to Indigo near O2 arena to see a comedy show.

I went to see Argentina vs Italy in Finalissima 2022 final, which was the last Euro winners vs Copa America winners, at Wembley stadium and saw Messi again star in the match.

In the summer of 2022 I went on a river canal boat trip from Camden.

Drashti and I went to London stadium in June 2022 stadium to see the Monster trucks event.

The same year, I saw the World Gymnastics Championships in Liverpool, the rescheduled Rugby League World Cup held in the UK. I went to see the England vs Australia wheelchair group match with my wife which was held in Copper Box, London in which a strong England side won.

My son, Yash, and I watched England vs Samoa in the men's rugby league semi-final at Emirates stadium in which the match tied at 26-all at full time and Samoa won with golden point.

I went to see the men's and women's rugby league World Cup final 2022 at Old Trafford, Manchester with my wife. It was a dominant Australia who won the World Cup final for men and women, and took the rugby league World Cup trophies home.

My wife and I also went to see the England vs France wheelchair rugby league World Cup 2022 final in Manchester in which England won to become world champions; the England player Jack Brown was outstanding.

In 2023, I went to see the All Elite Wrestling at Wembley stadium, Prince's Golf Club in Sandwich to watch the Women's amateur golf championships with my wife.

In August the same year I saw the Weeknd concert in Wembley stadium. My favourite Weeknd song is "I Feel It Coming" which he performed and I also like "Starboy".

I went to see West Ham vs Man City in 2023 and saw Erling Haaland play.

In April 2024 I went on the newly opened Big Ben tour with my wife and saw everything inside the Big Ben clock tower, climbing the many stairs inside.

I have also been many times to the Tower of London to see the crown jewels, especially the Kohinoor diamond, London Eye and Cable Car London near O2. I have on many occasions been to Victoria and Albert museum, British museum, Natural History museum, Science museum, Madam Tussauds, London Aquarium and once to London Transport museum and Kensington Palace.

At near Christmas time I went to Hyde Park's Winter Wonderland and Zippo Circus and many park funfairs. I also went with my wife to the Barbican conservatory which was also very good. On most of my trips I have stayed in beautiful 5-star hotels.

Horse racing grounds including Aintree for the Grand National 2012 and Cheltenham for the Cheltenham Gold Cup 2012 (in which I saw the legendary horse Kauto Star race), Kempton Park for King George VI race on boxing day, Royal Ascot, Sandown Park including coral eclipse race there, The Derby at Epsom, Glorious Goodwood racecourse and 1000 and 2000 guineas at Newmarket racecourse have been on my itinerary.

I have also been to various football grounds through the years including Wembley stadium where I saw many matches including Champions league final 2013 between Bayern Munich vs Borussia Dortmund and England vs Spain among others in 2011 when Spain were world champions and England won thanks to a Frank Lampard goal in which Spain totally dominated possession, Old Trafford, Arsenal new (Emirates stadium) and old (Highbury) including a 0-0 match there between Man Utd and Arsenal, Newcastle's St James's Park, Liverpool's Anfield, Man City's Etihad stadium, QPR's Loftus road, Charlton's Valley, Fulham's Craven Cottage, Chelsea's Stamford Bridge once to see Mourinho's Chelsea win 4-2 against Blackburn Rovers, Middlesbrough's Riverside Stadium, Celtic's stadium, Blackburn's Ewood Park in 2006 league cup semi-final against Man Utd, Tottenham's old (white hart lane) and new (Tottenham Hotspurs stadium) and went to the 2 test events when the new stadium opened for £5 ticket. Also, FA Cup tie and Premier League match against Brighton when Eriksen scored a late winner, winning 1-0, were to West Ham's London stadium, Brentford stadium, Watford's Vicarage Road game in hospitality package.

 I have seen many footballers in the football matches I went to including Iniesta, Xavi, Lampard, Rooney, Henry, etc. I have also visited Stonehenge.

 I have been to all the amusement parks in the UK including Thomas Land, Peppa Pig World, Nickelodeon Land, Alton Towers, Thorpe Park, Chessington and Lego Land.

Also, London Zoo, Centre Park, Brighton sky tower, Shrek's adventure in London, Woburn Safari Park, Longleat, Warner Brothers Studio in Watford, the proms at Royal Albert hall and HMS Belfast tour in London.

I have been to many concerts to see my favourite singers through the years, concerts including The Corrs, Backstreet boys, Britney Spears, Boyzone, Westlife, Ronan Keating, Hanson, etc. I am not much of the night clubbing type but I have been to a night club twice in Hammersmith, London.

I have also seen many theatre shows in London including Stomp and Mamma Mia to name two.

In one Polo match that I saw, the then Prince Charles was present.

I have been on a steam train in the UK in which coal is used as fuel for the train and the Orient Express train trip within London, which is like a Victorian age train, a unique experience.

I have been to Wimbledon tennis many times and Queens Club tennis in 2018 and saw Djokovic in the final that year. I have seen also Federer, Nadal, Djokovic, Andy Murray, Serena and Venus Williams all play live and I went to O2 arena many times to see the World ATP Tour Finals being played when they were held in London, Laver cup with Europe vs World in the tennis in 2022 on the last day of the tournament at O2 Arena and saw it from the boxes.

I have driven a Toyota Supra car and had various car driving experiences in the UK and driving on tracks including Porsche 911 turbo twice, Ferrari, Lamborghini, Bentley, Aston Martin and also a Formula 1 car on a circuit.

I went to see the London Lions play and win in basketball at Copper box arena once.

I have also seen just about every Bollywood and Hollywood film up to 2019. I have been to many cinemas in India and the UK. My favourite cinema in the UK is the one in O2 in North Greenwich.

I want to tell you about some X-rated things I have seen in my life. I have been to the Spearmint Rhino strip club in Park Royal, London when it was open there. I saw so many beautiful girls strip and do pole dances. In my lifetime I have been with about 50 call girls, paying them for one hour in-call at their place. The first time I used a call girl was in 2005 and the last time was in 2017.

What I did in my life is currently not possible unless you are rich, especially since there is a major cost of living crisis in which poor and middle- class people are struggling to survive.

I did this all with my own money by working in jobs. I was never a supervisor or managerial material but worked normal jobs primarily via agencies. Living with my parents I had nothing to pay and all the money I saved by working in jobs was mine to spend as I wished.

A fortunate and adventurous life, indeed!

www.ingramcontent.com/pod-product-compliance
Lightning Source LLC
Chambersburg PA
CBHW041311110526
44590CB00028B/4319